An Altruistic

Alex Andy Phuong

Contents

*Accepted by *Poets Choice Zine* on 07/16/19*
*Accepted by *The Academy of the Heart and Mind* on January 24, 2020*
(Previously published by different publications both online and in print)

Lifelong Education

School takes up many years
Yet those years must be spent
In order to Grow
Change
And Develop
Even after graduation
The educated can still undergo
Lifelong maturation
Learn something new daily
For self-empowerment

*Accepted by *Poets Choice* in response to the Writing Prompt "Nestled Lives" on 12/18/19.*
*Accepted by *The Academy of the Heart and Mind* on January 24, 2020*

Nestled Lives

Security vs. Simplicity
vs. Audacity
(but not recklessness)
Some might say
That they do not have
Enough time
But everyone does have time
It just depends on how
They spend it
Life is Fair
Yet "Life is not fair"
yet
"Life is fair"
It is just not always
In our favor
Ageing
Everlasting youth
might be the goal
of many
But ageing is a gift
Because age
Reveals how long
Someone has been alive
Whether or not such life
Could be Called
"A Nestled Life"

*Published on *The Academy of the Heart and Mind* on February 11, 2020*

Under the Influence

Under the Influence
Of Inspiration
Bridging gaps
Between generations
And establishing
Uniformed Unity
Across the Universe

*Published on *The Academy of the Heart and Mind* on February 11, 2020*

Revolt

Revolt against tyranny
Revolutionary Wars
Revolutionize Reality

Accepted by Sheila-Na-Gig online - Sheila-Na-Gig Under 30 on 1/12/20
*Reprinted on *The Academy of the Heart and Mind* on February 11, 2020*

Bold

Be audacious
Independent
Iridescent
Color the world
And paint over
What is dark

*Previously published in *Literary Yard* on February 27, 2020.*
https://literaryyard.com/2020/02/27/the-ultimate-stage/
*Reprinted on *The Academy of the Heart and Mind* on March 12, 2020.*

The Ultimate Stage

Social hierarchy
Filled with diversity
Colorful iridescence
Aesthetic decadence
There might be evil
in the world
but there is still hope
for the ones who dream
No matter how hard life may seem
Celebrate life and cheer for the dreamers
Pursuing passions respectfully

*This poem has been accepted for publication by *Poets Choice* on February 13, 2020.*
*Reprinted on *The Academy of the Heart and Mind* on March 9, 2020*

New Life

2020
New Decade
New Beginning
Years after graduation
But learning forevermore
Expressing gratitude for acquiring knowledge
Yet never forgetting what was taught in kindergarten
Play nice
Be nice
Do not judge books by their covers
(not to mention people)
Because a cover really is *not always* the book
Open eyes
Open hearts
Love myself selflessly
Be myself unapologetically
Never taking life so seriously
Because the real world is what it is
And that is the way of the world
And I am glad that I am a poet
Because my family and *true* friends know it!

*Published on *The Academy of the Heart and Mind* on February 11, 2020*

Peace Please

Piece the world together
By connecting the world
To establish a unified whole

*Published on *The Academy of the Heart and Mind* on February 11, 2020*

Frankly

Frankly I do not care what you say
I will let it go Because you never bothered me anyways

*Accepted by DSTL Arts – *Aurtistic Zine* on 9/12/19*
(Previously published by different publications both online and in print)

Much More Than *Rain Man*

Rain Man won "Best Picture"
Dustin Hoffman shed light
On what life is like
For autistics who have trouble
Perceiving and accepting reality
I am personally a fool who dreams
Related and relevant to MLK
Crazy as I may seem
Please do not say that I cannot
Because I am an autistic savant!

*Accepted by DSTL Arts – *Art Block Zine* on 9/03/19*
*Accepted by *The Academy of the Heart and Mind* on January 24, 2020*
(Previously published by different publications both online and in print)

Hustle and Bustle

Hustle and bustle
Living in Los Angeles
Is not *La La Land*

https://www.silentauctionsmagazine.com/poetry Accepted by *Silent Auctions Magazine* on January 19, 2020
*Published on *The Academy of the Heart and Mind* on February 11, 2020*

Underrepresentation

Minorities
Combined with
Congruence
Parallelism
Iridescence
Colors
Reflecting
Diversity
Trapped & bound,
but still bursting with freedom

*Previously published in *DSTL Arts – Aurtistic Zine*, accepted on 2/24/2020*

Never Speechless

Jasmine sang "Speechless"
    What is silent is NOT gold
Power to us all!

*Previously published in *DSTL Arts – Aurtistic Zine*, accepted on 2/24/2020*

Fight?

Fight for what is right?
Violence is not the answer
Practice Civil Disobedience
Thank you Thoreau

Previously published by Other Worldly Women Press and featured during the week of 3/23/20

Reverence

Never forget ancestry
Honor the past rather than dwell on it
Reverent
Fear not the revenant
Be Magnificent instead of malevolent
Don't hate; celebrate!
Remember respect
Especially self-respect

*Published on *The Academy of the Heart and Mind* on April 9, 2020*

Be Real

Reality might be bleak
Yet the ones who accept reality
Are not meek
For the strong
Are the ones who truly endure
And enjoy the gift of life itself

*Published by *The Academy of the Heart and Mind* on April 9, 2020*

Son Rise

Born into a world
Of night and day
Parents help a young man
Not go astray
Some abandon their families
Some start their own
Yet family under
The shining sun
Raises a person
To be mature

*Published on *The Academy of the Heart and Mind* on March 26, 2020*

Self

Individuality
is one element
Of Reality
Since there are many
People
That populate the world
Think of Others
Abandon selfishness
and improve yourself
By thinking,
"I can do this myself"

*Published on *The Academy of the Heart and Mind* on March 12, 2020*

The Light Ascending

Light in August
American landscape
The sun shines occasionally
Yet silver linings
Inspire
Hope
Positivity
Creativity
Shine the light
And aspire
To make the internal
Light shine through

*Published on *The Academy of the Heart and Mind* on March 12, 2020*

Playground

School days, School days
Playing during recess
Children do not necessarily
"Transform"
Into adults
Because age is simply a number
Feel the Earth beneath the feet
For aging is not obsolete
Because growing old is normal
Yet staying pure is optional
Choose goodness over evil
Like some of the greatest stories
Ever told
Be Bold!
(But also have fun along the way)
Why take life so seriously?
…seriously!
Have fun!

*Published on *The Academy of the Heart and Mind* on March 22, 2020*

Passages As Time Passes

Odes to beauty that fade throughout
The passage of time
Progression via maturation
Does time ever stop ticking?
Coping with the challenges that
Life has to offer
Yet life is the ultimate gift
because the world is our only home
"what sustains" is the present moment
Pave the path of where
We go in life
"I think, therefore I am."
So true…

*Accepted by *The Academy of the Heart and Mind* on March 28, 2020*

Towering Strength

Mountains and hills rise above the ground
Like how phoenixes rise above ashes
Phoenixes are mystical, magical, and symbolize rebirth
America wanted to separate from Europe
To become its own entity
Build upon the land of American soil
Because Gerald O'Hara asserted that, "Land is the only thing
that matters! It is the only thing that lasts!"
Leave your mark upon the world
Because time flies and life is short
One does not need to be as tall nor as high as a mountain
Because Dr. Seuss even said that, "A person is a person, no
matter how small"
Practice humbleness and humility
Instead of having a head full of hot air
And go ahead and let your voice be heard
Climb every mountain until dreams materialize like soil upon the
richness of Earth itself!

*Published on *The Academy of the Heart and Mind* on March 10, 2020*

Real Estate

Room
A Room of One's Own
Castles
Mansions
Apartments
Houses
Condos
Condominiums
Dorms
Dormitories
Duplex
School
Wuthering Heights
Thornfield
Pemberley
Tara
Manderley
Darlington Hall
Artificial Architecture
Imaginary
Physically
Spiritually
sublimely
House of Lancaster
House of York
The War of the Roses

Blending
Unifying
sanctuary
The White House
Earth
Home

*Accepted by *The Academy of the Heart and Mind* on March 26, 2020*

Musecal

Some kids like to read
and others do not

Some people are scientific
while others are prolific

Writers
Artists
Musicians
(and/or) dreamers

Dreams are much more than just nighttime phenomena
Because dreams make the phenomenal possible

Rhyme and reason
Sense and Sensibility
Tales as old as time
Poetry does not always need to rhyme

Imagination bears fruit
through the power of written language,
human thought,
and communication

If ideas pop up, write them down
Or else they could never be found

Take whatever side
Have the freedom to choose
Feel inspiration from a muse

Because fantasy can become reality
When people believe

*Accepted by *The Academy of the Heart and Mind* on March 28, 2020*

Fall

Fall season
Fall of Rome
Dark Ages
Renaissance
Reborn
The ones who pick themselves up
Fight against failure
And those who never try
Never truly live

*Accepted by *The Academy of the Heart and Mind* on April 6, 2020*

Stand Up

Stand straight
Stand tall
Avoid the Fall
of Rome
Stay strong
Courage is not
Foolish bravery
But the willingness
To keep going
Until peace returns

*Accepted by *The Academy of the Heart and Mind* on April 2, 2020*

Gaining and Giving Gratitude

Man
Manhood
Maturity
Fraternity
Maternity
Masculinity
Femininity
Gender Equality
Stand Up
Stay Strong
Never do wrong
Express Gratitude
For The One & Only Life

*Accepted by *The Academy of the Heart and Mind* on April 6, 2020*

Rhapsody

Rhapsodious Rhapsody
Embody
Mind
Body
Soul
A Celebration of
Artistic Creation
Exemplifying Humanness
And Hope for
Humanity

Originally published in *Museum Collection: an anthology of short stories and poetry*, edited by Alice Little, on December 4th, 2019.
Reprinted elsewhere on multiple publications

Museum

Physical buildings
And artistic architecture
Holding remnants from the past.
Museums hold artifacts
Yet artistic expression,
Hope
And creativity
Pave the way for the future.
This present moment in time
Is the greatest gift of all
Because it is, thankfully, not the last.

Stripes

Stripes might have a nice pattern,
but appearances can be deceiving.
The world and life itself are both black-and-white,
occasionally gray,
and sometimes as mature as *Fifty Shades of Grey*
Strip away deception
Utilize perception
To see the patterns
And beauty
All around
And simply accept
The fundamental fact
That all people have one
Single life
And that action
Must be taken
To help all that lives
On Earth
Our one and only home
Who will take a stand
And do what is right?
It is all up to
Personal Choice

Dare to Uphold the American Dream

Immigrants immigrating to escape conviction
Seeking new opportunities across the vastness of the sea
Is that "dream" even a real reality?
Declaring independence through the Declaration of Independence
The Fourth of July is a holiday
Or is it…?
Americanization/Westernization
Global dominance
The ideal is oftentimes too beautiful to be real
F. Scott Fitzgerald knew this when he wrote *The Great Gatsby*
and so did Arthur Miller when he staged the *Death of a Salesman*
The American Dream could really be a nightmare…
but while there is a life…there is hope…
Dream for a better tomorrow
No, do not dream…build, create, aspire, inspire
Because the world needs imagination for the sake of civilization

Restrictions of Propriety

Boundaries of propriety
Decimated and Dissipated
Borders might
Try to restrict
And restrain
Yet being free
Involves accepting
That life has no bounds
And letting the mind soar

World-Building

Civilization attempts to
Westernize the world
Through Collective Commodification
but no matter where people come from
nor how the world came into being
Every person is fundamentally human
Beings that belong together
In the naturally synthetic world

https://spillwords.com/avoiding-stagnation/
Firstly published in *Art Block Zine*; Volume 4, Issue 2: "Processing" in July 2019.

Avoiding Stagnation

Change is the only constant,
but only those willing to
change themselves
can make the world
a better place

https://spillwords.com/christmas-by-alex-andy-phuong/
Christmas

Christmas Day

Fun and play
Jovial holiday
Food and family
Mistletoe and holly
Jack Skellington misunderstood
but he still did the best he could
to spread Halloween fear
yet his intentions were still so dear
Dear family,
Spread love, not hate,
and let's all celebrate
for Christmas only comes once a year
and it is a time to rejoice with holiday cheer
Holy day and holy night
Let eternal love and light shine bright

13

Thirteen is a teen
Trick-or-Treat on Halloween
Then adulthood comes

Inspire with Fire

Heat
Fire
Passion
Love
Deception
Destruction
Think before you speak because words expressed with fiery
passion can never be revoked
We all have a figurative fire within us
Use it wisely for it impacts the world indefinitely

Bound

Borders might
Try to restrict
And restrain
Yet being free
Involves accepting
That life has no bounds

Buzz

What's the buzz?
What's the scoop?
What happened today?
Each day is a new day
and the past has gone astray
Time keeps on ticking
but speak loud and proud
For if voices are not heard
What is lost will never be found

Buzzy

Busy like a honeybee
Buzzy making noise
Instead of being cacophonic
Why not be nice and stay platonic?
Friendship can turn to love
Yet loving oneself must be true
For there is no one else in the world
Who is truly you

Borders of Diversity

Cultural identity
Occasional misunderstanding
Babel made it hard for people
To converse
Yet the language barrier curse
Could be reversed
If people unite
And Accept
The Borders of Diversity
And transcend those boundaries
To form a Gestalt

Just Ice

Excuse me, but could I please get a cup of "just ice"?
because ice was the reason why
a lot of people passed away
when the Titanic went astray
and paid the ultimate price
Unfortunately, some people really are just not nice
Celebrate instead of condemn the ones who demonstrate maturity
and honor those who came before
and the ones who strive for more
Live, laugh, love
Life itself!
Freedom, liberty, equality, and justice for all!
and actually, I do not need a cup of ice
for the cold never bothered me anyways

Young Nor Old

Age is simply a #
Because Behavior
Defines Character

Yourself

Mind the mind
Have a heart
Never part
From you or me
Celebrate individualism
Form harmonious unity
By changing yourself
Into nobility

Cope

No need to struggle
Overpower and overcome
To get "over it"
Addiction involves succumbing to
Desire
Yet being free involves breaking free

Transgression

Transgress, progress, regress
Digress, dig, exhume
Inspire, empower, achieve
Practice humility, humbleness, and
give generously
Sin might be sinful
but good and evil co-exist
Instead of transgressing
Strive to be a savior through the sanctification of salvation

Toil the Soil

Build upon the land of soil
Toil and work hard daily
Time on Earth is short
Life can be transparent
Some would serve
Others would not
Maybe they forgot?
About the beauty of life
Life might be meaningless
Yet it is the ultimate gift

Arrest

Cardiac arrest
might end life
but life itself is the greatest gift of all
Tests exist in life
To challenge character
Those who never try
Never pass
And failure is a myth
Because learning is
both constant
& continuous
As long as altruistic hearts unify,
Humanity can achieve indelible accomplishments
beneath the same blue sky

Transcendence

Diversity
Cognition
Kinesthetic
Auditory
Visual
Palpable Knowledge
Versatility
Multiplicity

Online Links

https://spillwords.com/author/alexandyphuong/

https://academyoftheheartandmind.wordpress.com/2020/02/11/poems-by-alex-andy-phuong/

http://alexandyphuongeng1492playlist.blogspot.com/

https://movieboozer.com/author/alex-phuong

https://mindfray.com/profile/Alex-Phuong/

http://www.short-humour.org.uk/10writersshowcase/10writersshowcase.htm#ANPH

Google "Alex Andy Phuong Carol Smallwood" for additional reviews and published collaborations with the Michigan-based author, Carol Smallwood

Alex Andy Phuong's poetic masterpiece previously published numerous times in countless journals and publications

Resisting Arrest

Uniting uniformed unity
You and I defy the sky
Team work and collaboration
Up to personal discretion
Civil Rights
Civility
Minorities against majorities
Stick to the status quo
But should we...?
Really?
Defy thy stars
And seek new avenues
Harness the power of creativity
And merge sense with sensibility
"Utopia" was conceived by Thomas More
But all must still must strive for more
For he was *A Man for All Seasons*
Arrests might be criminal
But people cannot be subliminal
If they want to break free
Listen to words of wisdom from me
"Know thyself, be thyself, harmoniously"